MONARCH

Shalamar Iris Outlaw

BookLeaf
Publishing

India | USA | UK

Presentation by *BookLeaf Publishing*

Web: www.bookleafpub.com

E-mail: info@bookleafpub.com

ISBN: 9789358318593

First edition 2023

DEDICATION

In honor of my daughter's legacy which is made complete in Christ.

Olivia,
I love you.
I miss you.
I mourn you.
Yet, I soldier on, holding tightly to the promise of an eternity with you in which we never say goodbye.

This book is also written for my son Tyler,

my husband Keith,

and for any of us who've turned our head toward the sky in a cry for help.

Salvation is here-

Jesus draws near.

ACKNOWLEDGEMENT

I want to acknowledge the Holy Spirit who gave
me utterance to this poem (in a matter of
minutes) one crisp autumn afternoon.

I want to acknowledge Jesus for the veracity of
my salvation.

And, in correlation with the sovereignty of the
triune God,
I want to acknowledge the great
I AM.

Who was,
Who is,
Who is to come.

PREFACE

Monarch /mŏn′ərk, -ärk″/

noun

1. A sole and absolute ruler.
2. A sovereign, such as a king.
3. One that commands or rules.
4. One that surpasses others in power or preeminence.
5. A species of butterfly.

The Caterpillar to the Butterfly: Part One

What does it look like
from way in the sky?
What it must feel like
to flutter and fly!

Such beauty-
Such purpose-
in all that you do,

The wind hits me differently
than it does you.

Way up there
it's airy,
it's thin,
you're complete.

Down here below,
I wriggle and creep.

No more to be found,
than to eat and to sleep.

The Butterfly to the
Caterpillar: Part Two

Oh, little worm,
I know you feel crushed.
And down there below,
the trudging is tough.
Each meal such a burden,
each movement so rough-

The Caterpillar to the Butterfly: Part Three

How do you know this?
How do you know?
What do you know of the things here below?
You dance upon flowers!
You stretch in the sun!
You soak in the splendor!
Down here there is none.

The Butterfly to the Caterpillar: Part Four

How can I know?
is the question you ask.
Since I revel in glory,
and in darkness you bask?

'Cause there was a season
I scurried like you
and believed in a promise
I hoped would come true:
That someday I'd morph
and become something new!

The Caterpillar to the Butterfly: Part Five

Hope.
What is *hope*?
I can't see what you see!
And down here below,
I see grubs just like me!
There's no hope below.
I am, so I know.

The Butterfly to the Caterpillar: Part Six

You don't see what I see,
you said it yourself-
I can see what's beyond
your little shelf.
You told me "I am."
Does that *name* ring a bell?

The Caterpillar to the Butterfly: Part Seven

The name of
I am?
Well, it started with me.
I've had it since consciousness,
'fore I could see!

The Butterfly to the
Caterpillar: Part Eight

You've had it dear worm
because there is another.
There is an I AM…
Who loves like a father,
a mother...
a brother…

The Caterpillar to the Butterfly: Part Nine

There is **no one** here,
I thought you could see.

They've gone.
I'm alone.
All that's left is just me.

The Butterfly to the Caterpillar: Part Ten

Look up little worm,
upon that cocoon-
The One, great I AM
was sealed in that tomb.

He went ahead.
He went instead.
Upon those twigs,
He made his bed.
He died.
He bled.

The Caterpillar to the
Butterfly: Part Eleven

That dreary thing?
Why, it's always been here.
It's creepy,
It's stained.
It fills me with fear!
I've heard the wind hiss to me,
"Don't you come near…"

The Butterfly to the Caterpillar: Part Twelve

That wasn't the wind,
Twas the snake all along!
He's been lurking in shadows
since the day you were born.
To get fat,
to feel safe,
to die here
in this storm.

The Caterpillar to the Butterfly: Part Thirteen

Oh no!
The rain comes.
I feel it at last!
What should I do?
It hurts!
Let's be fast.

The Butterfly to the Caterpillar: Part Fourteen

Get in! Get in **quick**!
Not a moment to waste.
I'll stall the old serpent,
I'm off!
Just *make haste*!

The Caterpillar to the Butterfly: Part Fifteen

I'm in
brother butterfly!
What should I do?
What must I say to turn out like you?!

.....

....

....

Hello?
Are you there?
Have you died in the storm?
My dear brother butterfly,
where have you gone?

The Caterpillar to **I AM**:
Part Sixteen

I AM?!
Are you there?
I'll cry out to you!
Please father-
please brother-
I want to be new!

I AM to the Caterpillar: Part Seventeen

Revelation 14:2 KJV "And I heard a voice from heaven, as the voice of many waters, and as the voice of a great thunder-"

"SO BE IT!"

The Butterfly to the Butterfly: Part One

Awake, little worm...
open your eyes.
What you now see
will be a surprise!
Not a worm,
but instead,
you are now
BUTTERFLY.

The Butterfly to the
Butterfly:
Part Two

My eyes can now see
the mountains, the bliss!
My wings feel the sunshine!
My God, what is this?!

I don't feel the sadness!
I don't fear the cold!
My body is new here,
not wrinkled.
not old.

I see it all clearly,
I see what you see…
The One,
The **I AM**
took my place on that tree,

So, that I could be free!

This marks THE END of the caterpillar's journey-

And the beginnings of a new life.

For more information on the author, her story, or Olivia Iris Outlaw, please visit:

www.girlnamedoutlaw.com

Or follow along on Instagram
@girlnamedoutlaw